Sweet Caroline Sweet

A Play

Tony Edwards

A SAMUEL FRENCH ACTING EDITION

SAMUEL FRENCH

FOUNDED 1830

SAMUELFRENCH-LONDON.CO.UK
SAMUELFRENCH.COM

CHARACTERS

Percy Middleditch, a bachelor. Early forties, bespectacled and slight of stature. Percy is one of life's losers. Although he is not stupid, everything about him—clothes, personality—is insignificant and neutral. "Office clerk" is stamped all over him. All his life people have trodden on or over him

Mrs Yates, forty-five to sixty. Percy's landlady. She is warm and sympathetic, with a genuine concern for Percy's welfare. She is also shrewd and able to speak her mind

Caroline Sweet, highly attractive. Beautifully groomed and dressed. Mid twenties to mid thirties, with the quiet, confident air that comes with being a bit special. Her intelligence matches her looks i.e. pushing Mensa!

Mr Gillis, estate agent. Pushy and eager to please. Any age. Could be a female role.

The action takes place in the lounge of Percy's flat and later in a room of his new flat

Time—the present

PRODUCTION NOTES

The time span covered by the play is about six weeks. The period of time which elapses between "scenes" ranges from one hour to a few weeks. These intervals are covered by black-outs, during which the characters change clothes, positions, etc., and items in the room are removed or put into place as necessary.

All changes should be kept to a minimum, thus keeping the intervals as short as possible. Percy is most affected, particularly with changes of clothes and mood, but with efficient back stage support, his progress through the play can be made very smooth and effective.

The biggest interval will be the changing of rooms—essential in the plot—so keep furniture as simplistic as you feel you can cope with. While the two-seater settee must be changed, why not use the same table with a large cloth on it? With proper planning, all movements and changes are far simpler than they appear on the page.

So be bold, be positive, and please—enjoy it!

T.E.

SWEET CAROLINE SWEET

Curtains open on to a neatly but simply furnished room. Along the back wall is a stereo unit and a sideboard, on which are a telephone and directory and in which are drinks and glasses, pen and paper. A table flanked by two chairs is US. *A two-seater sofa is* DS. *Other furniture at director's discretion. The "doors" of the room are off stage between the flies. The bedroom is* USL. *The kitchen is* DSL. *Entrances and exits are made* USR.

A door is heard to slam. Percy Middleditch enters. He is wearing an overcoat and is carrying a brief-case. He is upset and angry. He bangs his brief-case on to the table, goes straight to the sideboard and pours himself a whisky. He downs it in one. He pours another and sits down at the table, fists clenched, drinking. There is a knock at the door. He quickly tries to compose himself

Percy Eh ... come in, Mrs Yates.

Mrs Yates enters, smiling and looking eager

Mrs Yates I heard you come in, Mr Middleditch, and couldn't wait to know. Did you get it?

Percy sniffs himself back to normality

Percy No. No, I'm afraid not, Mrs Yates.

Mrs Yates Oh, Mr Middleditch! I'm so sorry. You were so sure.

Percy Obviously I shouldn't have been.

Mrs Yates But why not? What happened?

Percy A young ... young whippersnapper. Only two years with the firm. That's what happened!

Mrs Yates That doesn't sound fair.

Percy Fair! They don't know the meaning of the word! His two years against my eighteen. I taught him all he knows.

Mrs Yates But they promised ...

Percy Not exactly promised, Mrs Yates, but they certainly gave me the impression that I was to get it—but what did I get today? "The job needs flair and drive, Mr Middleditch—new ideas, ambitious thinking". What was it he said? Oh yes, "We need to tap the energy and zeal of youth, Mr Middleditch. You do understand, don't you?" Yes, I understand all right! Experience counts for nothing. You have to be a whizz kid bent on changing the world by tomorrow lunchtime to get anywhere these days. God knows what happened to rewards for loyalty, respect ...

Mrs Yates It's a shame—a crying shame. If anyone deserves promotion it's you. (*Pause*) Look love, at least take your coat off. (*She helps him*) You stay there and I'll make you a nice cuppa. That's what you need. I'll put the kettle on.

Mrs Yates exits to the kitchen

Percy gets up, pours himself another drink and sits down again

Mrs Yates enters

Mrs Yates There. Won't be long. (*She sits at the table*) What are you doing about your meal tonight?
Percy Um ... nothing. I'm not hungry.
Mrs Yates You've got to eat. I've got a mince on. It only needs a couple more spuds and ...
Percy No, really, Mrs Yates, thank you, but I couldn't eat a thing.
Mrs Yates Well, it's understandable, I suppose. (*Pause*) You need cheering up. Why don't you go out to the pictures or the theatre tonight? It'll take your mind off things.
Percy No, really ...
Mrs Yates Where's your paper?
Percy Oh, I forgot to stop off. I wasn't thinking ...
Mrs Yates Of course. I'll go and get mine. (*She turns at the door*) I'll tell you what. It'll be my treat!

She exits

Percy gets up and starts pouring another drink

Mrs Yates enters, takes the bottle from Percy and gives him the paper

Mrs Yates Tea's better for you than that stuff. You look at the paper. The kettle should have boiled by now.

She exits to the kitchen

(*Off*) Nothing like a good cup of tea at a time like this.

Percy sits down at the table

  Mrs Yates brings him in a cup of tea

There, get that down you.
Percy Thanks, Mrs Yates.

She takes the paper and opens it

Mrs Yates Let's have a look at what's on. There's that new spy thriller on at the Embassy. Fancy that? Or what about the musical at ...
Percy I don't really feel like going out, thanks all the same.
Mrs Yates You should, love. You shouldn't sit here brooding by yourself. It's not good for you. You need company when you're feeling *down*—helps to cheer you *up*. You should make more friends.
Percy Friends? Not my strong point, I'm afraid.
Mrs Yates But why not, love?
Percy Don't know really. Everyone I meet seems to be too young, too old, too loud—too ambitious. I'm not blaming them. It's me. I'm the misfit.
Mrs Yates 'Course you're not, love! You should find a nice girl. Get out of the flat more. Enjoy yourself.
Percy Don't worry about me, Mrs Yates. I'm all right.

Mrs Yates sighs, shakes her head and gets up

Mrs Yates Sure you don't want some mince?
Percy No thanks, really.
Mrs Yates Give us a shout if you change your mind—and I am sorry, love.
Percy Yes. Thanks, Mrs Yates.

  She exits

Percy takes his tea and paper to the settee. He is a little wobbly. He sits and reads, drinking his tea. He comes to an item of interest, folds the paper and studies it. It's an advertisement. He reads it out loud

Percy "Man, fifty-two, looking for attractive woman of similar age with view to long term company and friendship ..."

He thinks, then with a chuckle discards the idea. He gets up, takes the paper and the tea cup and puts them on the table. He gets another whisky and wanders back to the table. He sits, sipping his drink, then looks at the paper again. He is getting rather drunk. He giggles and decides

If a fifty-two year old can do it, so can I! What have I got to lose, anyway? (*He finishes his drink, gets paper and pen from the sideboard, sits down again and writes*) "Man, forty-one, seeks female companion . . .

There is a slow fade to Black-out to denote a passage of time

It is one week later. Mrs Yates is dusting and tidying the room. Percy is heard to call to her from off stage

Mrs Yates I'm in your room, love.

Percy enters, excited and nervous. He quickly takes off his overcoat and puts his case and paper on the table. He takes a letter from his inside pocket

Had a good day?
Percy Fine, thanks. Mrs Yates, do you remember last week when you told me I needed more friends—to get out more?
Mrs Yates Oh yes, you were very low.
Percy Well, that night, I put an advertisement in the local paper.
Mrs Yates Advertisement? What sort of an advertisement?
Percy For a . . . well, for a . . . friend . . . a girl friend!
Mrs Yates You mean the Lonely Hearts column?
Percy Eh . . . yes.
Mrs Yates Good Lord!
Percy I would never have done it without the whisky!
Mrs Yates Did you get any replies?
Percy Three. One was sixteen and one was nineteen. It sounded as if they both had the problems of the world to solve, but this came this morning!

He gives her the letter. She reads to herself

Mrs Yates My, she sounds very nice—and she's coming round this evening! Well done, Mr Middleditch!
Percy Yes, but I don't know what to—do!

Mrs Yates You'll be all right. Are you going to take her out?
Percy I don't know. I suppose so. What do you think?
Mrs Yates I think that would be very nice. Go out for a meal and
  have a chat. Get to know each other.
Percy Yes. Right. Yes. Well, that's what we'll do then.
Mrs Yates And relax love!
Percy But what if she doesn't like me?
Mrs Yates Then you put another ad. in the paper tomorrow!
  Don't worry, she'll like you. Look, it says early evening. That
  could be any time. Go and get yourself ready—and good luck.

She ushers him towards his bedroom

Percy Yes. Right. Eh, thank you, Mrs Yates.

*Mrs Yates smiles and takes a few moments to tidy bits and pieces in
the room*

She exits

*After a pause Percy enters from bedroom. He has no shoes on. He
is also shirtless, but wears a vest. He is wiping his face with a
towel. He goes into the kitchen and returns with a shirt on a
hanger. He starts to put the shirt on. While doing so he exits to the
bedroom, and returns putting his tie on—looking in the mirror on
the "fourth" wall. He stops halfway through tying his tie and
starts to stuff his shirt into his trousers. There is a knock on the
door. He freezes, then panics, trying to do everything at once, but
getting nowhere. Another knock. He realizes he must open the
door, and in disarray does so*

Caroline enters.

*She walks into the room, looks briefly round, then turns to face
Percy. Percy is so taken by her appearance he is motionless,
gawping. The shirt, tie and shoes are forgotten. Caroline smiles*

Caroline Hello. It's Percy, isn't it?

Percy breaks out of his paralysis, still trying to sort himself out

Percy Eh, yes. I'm very sorry to be in such a state. I got home
  from work late—the traffic. Oh, please sit down. Can I give you
  ... get you anything? I don't ...

Caroline puts her hands on his shoulders. He stops jumping about

Caroline I'll sort the tie out. You tackle the trousers!

Percy dumbly tucks his shirt in while Caroline does up his tie. As they each finish their task, Caroline holds her hand out. They shake hands

Caroline Hi. I'm Caroline. Caroline Sweet.
Percy Eh, yes, of course—you wrote. I'm Percy Middleditch. It's a silly name. I've never liked it.
Caroline It's—unusual.
Percy Have a drink. I've only got Scotch, vodka or sherry.
Caroline A sherry will be fine, thank you.

She sits on the sofa. He gets the drinks, looks at the sofa, and brings a chair from the table and sits. She smiles at his nervousness

Cheers. Here's to getting to know you.
Percy Yes. Cheers. (*He downs his drink in one*)
Caroline Do you live here alone, Percy?
Percy Yes. Well, of course, there are others in the block—but in the flat here, yes.
Caroline It's very nice. Comfortable.
Percy Yes. Another drink?
Caroline Not yet, thanks. What are your plans for the evening?
Percy Plans? Ah, yes, well, I thought we might go out—that's if you want to—for a meal—or to the pictures if you'd rather.
Caroline A meal sounds fine. Did you have a restaurant in mind?

Percy looks blank

Percy Restaurant? Um, well I don't really know. I'm sorry, I'm not very good at . . . I don't normally go to restaurants and . . .
Caroline Don't worry. I know a lovely place. Quiet and inexpensive.
Percy That sounds fine.

Mrs Yates knocks and enters. Caroline gets up

Mrs Yates How are you getting on, love? Are you . . . ooh, I'm so sorry. I didn't realize your company had arrived. Do excuse me . . .

Her voice trails off as she takes Caroline in

Percy That's all right, Mrs Yates. Come on in and meet Caroline.

Caroline, this is my good friend Mrs Yates. She's my landlady. She lives across the hall. Mrs Yates, this is Caroline Sweet.

Caroline (*shaking hands*) Hello, Mrs Yates.

Mrs Yates Hello, love.

Caroline You're not as alone as you say you are, Percy.

Percy Pardon?

Caroline I have a feeling Mrs Yates keeps a very good eye on you.

Mrs Yates I do a bit of cleaning and things for him. Make sure he doesn't starve. You know what men are when left to their own devices.

Caroline I think he's very lucky.

Mrs Yates I do my best. Are you local, Miss Swee . . . Caroline?

Caroline Oh yes. I live opposite Carlton Cosmetics, which is very handy since I work there.

Mrs Yates Oh, nice.

Percy What do you do there, Caroline?

Caroline I'm in the Sales Office. Promotions Manager.

Mrs Yates Oh, very nice. Eh, look, you two. Are you going out tonight?

Percy Yes. We're going for a meal.

Mrs Yates Well, off you go then! You should be finding out about each other over a dinner table, not here. Go on. I'll close the door.

Caroline Right you are, Mrs Yates. Ready Percy?

Percy Yes, of course.

He grabs his coat and makes for the door

Caroline Percy.

Percy Yes?

Caroline Wouldn't you feel more comfortable with shoes on?

Percy smiles sheepishly and runs into the bedroom. He re-emerges hopping, trying to put his shoes on as he goes

He finally manages it. Caroline and Mrs Yates smile knowingly to each other

Goodnight, Mrs Yates. Hope to see you again soon.

Percy and Caroline exit

Mrs Yates has a suggestion of a frown on her face as she looks around the room

She shrugs and exits

There is a slow fade to Black-out

It is a few days later. The lights come up on an empty room. Pause

   A knock is heard and Mrs Yates enters

Mrs Yates Cooee! Are you home yet, Mr Middleditch?

No reply. She does a bit of tidying and dusting, then sees a card on the sideboard. She picks it up

   (*Reading*) Thank you for a wonderful evening. Here's to many more. Lots of love, Caroline. Kiss, kiss, kiss!

   Percy enters and sees her

Percy Hello, Mrs Yates.
Mrs Yates (*jumping*) Ooh, Mr Middleditch. I didn't hear you come in.

Percy takes off his coat

Percy The door was open.
Mrs Yates Yes, I had the kettle on and came to see if you wanted a cuppa. What must you think of me—reading your card!
Percy I don't mind.
Mrs Yates I haven't seen you for a couple of days and wondered ... well, you know ... how things were going?

Percy flings his arms wide

Percy Things, Mrs Yates, are wonderful! Life is wonderful! Work is wonderful! This flat is wonderful! That card is wonderful! You, Mrs Yates are wonderful! But most of all—Caroline is wonderful!
Mrs Yates Why, Mr Middleditch! I've never seen you like this before.
Percy That's because I've never been like this—felt like this before! Caroline is so ... she is ...
Mrs Yates Wonderful?
Percy (*laughing*) Yes—that does sort of sum it up.
Mrs Yates I'm so pleased for you, love. So you've been having a good time?

Percy Mrs Yates. In only two nights I've done things I never thought I'd ever do. Dancing! Can you imagine me on a dance floor? Yet dancing with Caroline . . . I feel I've been dancing all my life! We've been to a theatre, two restaurants and a dance hall . . .

Mrs Yates All in two nights?

Percy . . . and tonight it's a concert.

Mrs Yates So who's the misfit now?

Percy I know. I never thought it possible. I'm living in a different world.

Mrs Yates And it sounds an expensive one.

Percy Expensive? Not at all. I'm not short of a few pennies, but Caroline has insisted on paying her way from the start. She's . . .

Both Wonderful!!!

They both laugh. Percy calms down to a quieter mood. They both sit at the table

Percy Mrs Yates, do you know what it means to have someone who listens—really listens—to what you say? Someone who asks for your advice, your opinions? It's never happened to me before. For the first time I feel . . . she makes me feel, as if I . . . matter! She sort of . . . sort of fits into my mind, Mrs Yates. Do you know what I mean? Like dovetailing. She's special, Mrs Yates. Very, very special.

Mrs Yates She sounds almost too perfect.

Percy Eh?

Mrs Yates I had my doubts at first . . . but no, you're obviously enjoying yourself . . .

Percy Doubts?

Mrs Yates Well, love. I just don't want you to get hurt. Don't build things up too quickly, too soon.

Percy What do you mean?

Mrs Yates Look, love. She is a very beautiful woman and . . .

Percy Oh, I see. And you were wondering what a girl like that sees in a bloke like me?

Mrs Yates Well, love. I must confess the thought did cross my mind.

Percy I'm not that stupid, Mrs Yates. It crossed my mind as well. So, I actually said to her, "What does a girl like you see in a bloke like me?" And do you know what she said?

Mrs Yates What did she say?

Percy She looked me straight in the eye and said, "I can rest with you, Percy."

Mrs Yates Eh?

Percy I know. I didn't understand at first. But she explained. You see, she had been with all the playboy types. You know—fast cars and late nights. Getting up after lunch. How can people live like that? Anyway, all she got from them was pressure. Social pressure, eh ... sexual pressure—all "parties and panic" as she put it! So she looked for a more genuine relationship—but it was difficult. The quiet types were scared off by her looks, so she decided to make the first move. Through the Lonely Hearts column of the paper.

Mrs Yates I've read about that.

Percy What?

Mrs Yates Lovely girls, you know, actresses and that—being lonely because the boys think they're unattainable.

Percy Yes. That's exactly what happened to Caroline. Now she says she feels more relaxed and comfortable. She says I'm ... eh, I'm just the type she's been looking for—and I'm certainly not arguing!

Mrs Yates Quite right, love. You enjoy yourself while you can.

Percy looks at his watch

Percy Talking of which I've got to get ready. We're off to a concert tonight. Beethoven. She loves Beethoven.

Mrs Yates Beethoven's your favourite.

Percy I know. Wonderful, isn't it!

He exits into the bedroom humming Beethoven

Mrs Yates Amazing!

Mrs Yates does some more tidying up, muttering and shaking her head in disbelief

She exits

There is a slow fade to Black-out

The Lights come up. It is one hour later

Percy, dressed to go out, enters from the bedroom with a box which he puts on the table. He fiddles with his tie

There is a knock on the door

Percy It's open.

Caroline enters. Percy picks up the box, goes to her and kisses her on the cheek

Hello darling. I've been thinking of you all day. I've got something for you.

Caroline takes the box. She is noticeably subdued

Caroline Thank you, Percy. That's very sweet of you.

Percy laughs loudly

Percy Oh, very good! "Very sweet". They're chocolates! To eat at the concert.

Caroline smiles thinly. She doesn't move

Eh, ready then?
Caroline Is there time for a drink before we go?

Percy looks at his watch

Percy Well, yes—if we make it a quick one. Sherry?
Caroline Scotch.

Percy looks a little surprised, then pours two drinks

Percy Here's to . . . dear old Beethoven.

Caroline sips her drink, saying nothing. Percy now realizes she is unusually quiet

Eh, there's nothing wrong, is there?
Caroline I thought I might give it a miss tonight.
Percy What, the concert?
Caroline Yes.
Percy (*disappointed*) Oh. Well, all right. If you would rather stay in.
Caroline I mean the whole evening.
Percy What?
Caroline I wouldn't be very good company.

Percy But why? What's the matter? Is something wrong?
Caroline No. It's just that I don't feel too good—rather be by myself. I'm sorry.
Percy Can I get you anything? An aspirin or something?
Caroline No. It's nothing like that.
Percy So there is something!
Caroline Percy, please, I don't want to talk about ...
Percy About what? Caroline, I want to help if I can.
Caroline It's got nothing to do with you, Percy. It's ... all right, it's a problem, but I'll sort it out.
Percy "A problem shared is a problem halved". Give me my half!
Caroline I've got to work it out for ...

She starts to cry. Percy is full of concern, but doesn't know how to react. He holds her awkwardly

Percy There, there, don't cry. Tell me what's wrong. I'll help. I'll do anything—you know that.
Caroline Dear Percy, you're so sweet, so kind. I'm sorry to make all this fuss over a few poun ...
Percy Money? Is it money?
Caroline I'm sorry. I didn't mean to say that.
Percy Is it?
Caroline Yes. It's money, but I am not involving you in ...
Percy Tell me. Then we'll decide if I can help or not.
Caroline But ...
Percy I insist!

Caroline looks at him for a moment, then decides

Caroline All right—but it's still my problem.
Percy Yes. Go on.
Caroline Well, a few months ago my sister bought a car ...
Percy I didn't know you had a sister.
Caroline My younger sister. She lives just outside Manchester. She bought this car on H.P. and because of her age, she needed a guarantor. At the time there were no problems. She was earning good money and expected to pay it off in a couple of years.
Percy What happened?
Caroline The company she worked for went bust. Simple as that. She couldn't get another job and fell behind with her payments. So it's down to the guarantor—namely me.

Percy How much?

Caroline Look Percy, forget it. You are . . .

Percy Caroline. How much?

Caroline Two thousand pounds.

Percy Wow! But why doesn't the finance company just take the car back?

Caroline Because the silly little idiot has done a bunk. No one knows where she is.

Percy Oh. Can't you arrange payments over a period of . . .

Caroline They want the lot—and now. Well, two weeks to be exact. After I got their letter this morning I rang them to try to sort something out. No way! Under these circumstances they want their money back fast.

Percy And you can't pay?

Caroline Not on their terms. I'd have to sell everything I own to . . .

She cries again, he comforts her

Percy Hey, come on. Enough of that. Didn't I tell you I was a millionaire!

Caroline Please, Percy. It's not funny.

Percy Of course it is!

Caroline Percy!

Percy You haven't got a problem, because I've got two thousand pounds!

Caroline is open mouthed

Caroline Percy! Oh no! Oh no you don't! You are not paying a penny.

Percy In fact, I've got a darned sight more than two thousand pounds. Look, I'm not exactly famous as a playboy. All the money I've earned over the years has gone straight into the bank. The thought of it doing some good is more than welcome—especially as it will be helping you.

Caroline goes to him and kisses him

Caroline Dear Percy, thank you for wanting to help me, but there's more to it than that. I have my pride, you know. I've never borrowed a penny in my life and I don't intend to start now—but thanks anyway.

Percy OK. So what's the alternative?
Caroline Um ... well ...
Percy Come on. What are you going to do?
Caroline I honestly don't know yet—but I'll find a way. My firm
    might give me a loan ...
Percy Is that likely?
Caroline No, no it's not, but ...
Percy Caroline, listen to me. You have a very real problem that
    needs a quick solution. I have that solution; so tomorrow
    morning I am going to the bank to draw out two thousand
    pounds which I will give you tomorrow night ...
Caroline But ...
Percy But nothing. I *want* to do it. Please—don't deprive me of
    the pleasure of helping you.

Caroline falls sobbing into Percy's arms

Caroline I can't believe it! I just can't believe it!

Percy is now in charge

Percy Come on. Dry those eyes. We've got a date with Beethoven,
    remember. Where's your hanky?
Caroline In my bag.

*The bag is on the table. Percy picks it up and a gun falls out. Percy is
astonished. He picks up the gun and looks at Caroline questioningly.
She is not concerned*

Caroline Be careful. It's loaded.

*She takes it from him and puts it back in the bag. She takes out her
hanky and blows her nose*

Percy A loaded gun?
Caroline You'd be surprised how many girls carry them these
    days. I would never be without it.
Percy Bit extreme, isn't it?

Caroline looks him in the eye

Caroline You could say that describes what happens to girls who
    get caught by some ...
Percy Yes, of course. I see what you mean.

Caroline smiles and puts her arms around his neck

Caroline Percy darling—I just don't know what to say.

Her closeness makes him nervous again. He laughs weakly

Percy Eh—just say you'll hurry. Beethoven's waiting.

They both laugh, link arms and exit

There is a slow fade to Black-out

It is two evenings later. Mrs Yates enters from the kitchen with two cups of tea

Mrs Yates What time did you say she was coming?
Percy (*off*) Seven. What time is it now?
Mrs Yates Nearly eight.

Percy enters from the bedroom

Percy I'm worried, Mrs Yates. Something has happened to her.
Mrs Yates Well give her a ring.
Percy Actually, I don't know her number. She said she was ex-directory. She has a flatmate who didn't want people ... anyway, I've never had any cause.
Mrs Yates Then pop over to see her. If she comes after you've gone, I'll send her ...
Percy You're not going to believe this, Mrs Yates.
Mrs Yates What?
Percy I don't know her address, either.
Mrs Yates What! You must do. You take her home, don't you?
Percy Yes, and drop her off outside the block of flats. She's trying to get rid of this flatmate and it wouldn't help if ...

Mrs Yates is astounded

Mrs Yates You've never been in for ... a coffee ... or ... anything?
Percy No.
Mrs Yates Blimey.
Percy I hope it isn't her sister's car.
Mrs Yates Pardon?
Percy She's having to sort out a problem about money owed on her sister's car.
Mrs Yates I'm still not with you.

Percy Her sister absconded with a car on H.P. and Caroline has been left holding the bill. I was able to help her out, and I'm just wondering . . .

Mrs Yates What do you mean, "help her out"?

Percy I lent her some money so that she . . .

Mrs Yates Wait! Wait—just a minute, love. Let me get this right. You lent her some money?

Percy Yes.

Mrs Yates When?

Percy Last night.

Mrs Yates Do you mind if I ask you how much?

Percy Of course not. Two thousand pounds.

Mrs Yates realizes what has happened. She sits heavily

Mrs Yates Oh my God, no! You poor man!

Percy What's the matter, Mrs Yates?

Mrs Yates Oh Mr Middleditch—can't you see?

Percy See what?

Mrs Yates Oh love, think about it. No phone number, no address—no trace!

Percy What are you saying?

Mrs Yates is reluctant to utter the words, but does

Mrs Yates You've been conned, love. You've been taken for two thousand pounds!

Percy tries to take this information in, but can't

Percy No. Don't be silly, Mrs Yates. Caroline wouldn't do that.

Mrs Yates Has she ever been late before?

Percy No—but that could be for all sorts of . . .

Mrs Yates She was after your money! All those evenings—everything was a build-up to that.

Percy thinks again, but still does not accept it

Percy No, I don't believe that. (*Then defensively*) In fact, she didn't want to tell me about the money at first. I dragged it out of her—and then she wouldn't accept anything. It was me who made her take it.

Mrs Yates Which proves just how clever she was. Phone Carlton Cosmetics.

Percy What?
Mrs Yates See if she really works there.
Percy Look, Mrs Yates. There is no way that . . .
Mrs Yates Please, love. For your own sake.

Percy sits defiantly

Percy No! I'm not going to listen to this. Anyway, it's too late to
  phone.
Mrs Yates They work twenty four hours a day—shift work.
  Phone them.
Percy No.
Mrs Yates Then I will!

She looks up the number and dials

Hello? Carlton Cosmetics? Good evening. Sorry to phone so
late, but I'm preparing some papers to send to your Company
and need Miss Caroline Sweet's extension number to check a
detail. She's in the Sales Office—Promotions Manager. Pardon?
Yes, I appreciate there is no one there now. I just need the
number. Yes, thank you—I'll hold.

Percy is now sitting on the edge of his chair

Hello? Extension three five eight . . . What's that? . . . Oh, who is
it then? . . . Mrs Avril Mason. You've never heard of a Caroline
Sweet . . . Oh, well yes, you would, wouldn't you . . . I'll update
our records. Thanks for your help. Goodbye.

*Percy's eyes are imploring her to tell him it's not true. She puts the
phone down*

(*Quietly*) That was the Senior Security Officer. He's been with
the firm for fifteen years. There has never been a Caro . . .

Percy jumps up, desperate

Percy He's wrong! He must be!
Mrs Yates No, love. He isn't.

Percy sinks back into the chair

I'm sorry, love. Is there anything I can get you?

Percy doesn't move

No, all right. I'll phone the police from my place.

Percy jerks into motion

Percy Police?
Mrs Yates Of course. You must report . . .
Percy No police.
Mrs Yates But Mr Middl . . .
Percy No police!
Mrs Yates All right, love. If you say so. I'll look in tomorrow. Get
   a good night's . . .

   She trails off and exits

*Percy sits silently for a few moments. Slowly his body shakes and he
sobs, quietly at first, but then louder as anger and frustration build
up. He gets up and attacks the room—throwing, kicking, sobbing.
He finally slumps at the table, banging his fist on it. The words are in
time with the thumping*

Percy Bitch! Bitch! Bitch! Bitch! Bitch!

There is a slow fade to Black-out

*It is the following morning. Percy, now calm, is dialling with a
newspaper at his elbow*

Percy Hello? Gillis and Wade? Good morning. I see you are
   advertising flats on short term lets. Yes. It sounds just the sort of
   thing I'm looking for. It also says immediate possession—so
   how quickly could one . . . yes . . . yes . . . good . . . so it could be
   as quick as two weeks? Good. In that case, I'd like to make an
   appointment to see some. Well, today, if possible. That's fine, at
   your offices. Middleditch—and you are?—Mr Gillis. Two-
   thirty. Yes . . . and thank you for fitting me in. Yes . . . goodbye,
   Mr Gillis.

*He sits and looks at the mess from the previous night, then starts to
clear it up. There is a knock on the door, and Mrs Yates enters*

Mrs Yates Hello, Mr Middleditch. Eh, are you OK?
Percy Yes, don't worry, Mrs Yates I'm fine. (*He indicates the
   mess*) All emotions spent, so to speak. Back to normal.
Mrs Yates You're not going into work today?

Percy No.

Mrs Yates Oh good. I think that's wise. Here, let me help.

Percy Thanks, and thanks for last night.

Mrs Yates What?

Percy Phoning like you did. Making me realize.

Mrs Yates That's all right, love.

Percy I've been doing some phoning of my own this morning.

Mrs Yates Oh?

Percy Yes. I re-checked with Carlton Cosmetics—with their personnel department, and you were right, of course. Caroline has never worked there. Then I rang the police.

Mrs Yates But last night you said . . .

Percy I couldn't think straight then. I imagined Caroline in prison . . . you know, but I realized I had to report it—for what it was worth.

Mrs Yates Why—what did they say?

Percy They said they couldn't do anything.

Mrs Yates What? Why not?

Percy They confirmed it was a con. In fact it's not particularly unusual. These women are professionals. That's why she was such a good actress—so convincing. God when I think of the things she said—and the way she said them! Anyway, they prey on the Lonely Hearts columns for likely . . . victims. But even if she was traced, she would maintain that it was a genuine relationship that went sour. She would then claim that I gave her the money as a gift—and I wouldn't be able to prove otherwise. No paperwork or signatures.

Mrs Yates But surely the police know . . .

Percy Knowing and proving are two different things.

Mrs Yates So she's got away with it?

Percy Looks like it. Not a bad way to make a living is it? Wine and dine with someone for two to three weeks, and end up with two thousand pounds—tax free!

Mrs Yates It's criminal!—well, you know what I mean.

Percy (*laughing*) Yes, I know what you mean.

Mrs Yates I must say you're taking it very calmly, after last . . .

Percy Yes. I'll be going away on holiday in two or three weeks time—you know, have a break. I'll let you know the details later.

Mrs Yates What a good idea. Get away from it all for a while.

Percy Yes—get away from it all.

There is slow fade to Black-out

The lights come up on the new flat. It is three weeks later

Percy and Mr Gillis enter. Mr Gillis is speaking

Gillis ... and you'll see that that bit of decorating has been done
in the bedroom, the overflow in the cistern is OK now. They've
ironed out the knocking in the central heating and ... oh, what
was the other thing? Oh yes, the phone is connected. (*He gives
Percy the keys*) All yours, Mr Middleditch.
Percy Thank you, Mr Gillis.
Gillis I'm sure you'll find it a very pleasant abode, sir. The last
tenants were very happy here. They always ...
Percy Yes, I'm sure they were.
Gillis Of course ... well, I'll be off then.
Percy Thank you for your help.
Gillis My pleasure. If there's anything I can do ...
Percy I'll let you know.
Gillis Yes, well, goodbye.
Percy Goodbye, Mr Gillis.

Mr Gillis exits

*Percy takes his coat off and sits at the table. He opens his briefcase
and takes out writing paper and envelope. He writes, reading aloud
as he does so*

Percy Male, aged ... um ... forty-eight. Own flat, own car.
Would like to meet female ...

There is a slow fade to Black-out

*It is a few weeks later. Percy is sitting reading a paper. There are two
drinks already prepared and two letters on the table. The door bell
rings. He looks at his watch. He gets up and puts on a pair of horn-
rimmed spectacles. He goes to the door. Just before he opens it he
starts to cough, so that when he opens the door, his hand is covering
his lower face. Caroline enters. As she passes him he turns and stops
coughing. As she turns towards him he takes off the spectacles*

Caroline My God—Percy!
Percy Hello, Caroline.
Caroline What are you . . . oh, my God!

She appears more annoyed than frightened

Percy Sit down.
Caroline Look Percy . . .
Percy Sit down!

She does. Percy gives her one of the prepared drinks

Percy Here's to . . . what shall we drink to?

Caroline is silent

Seeing each other again? No? Two thousand pounds?
Caroline Percy, please! How did you . . .
Percy Find you? It was really very simple. Just a little time and
patience—both of which I have in ample supply. I knew where
you—plied for your trade. So I advertised in all the local papers,
and some out of town in case you had moved. To every reply I
sent a photo—of someone else, of course. It took a few weeks,
but you finally got caught in the net.

He picks up the two letters and waves them

I just compared your handwriting with your original letter—and
here we are! I'm only surprised it hasn't been done before.
Caroline It has, but it's rare.
Percy Because your victims are too ashamed?
Caroline Most can afford it and write it off.
Percy The money, yes—but what about feelings, Caroline? How
do you assess the value of feelings?

Caroline sips her drink

Caroline What do you want me to say?
Percy Well, what about the sweet nothings you whispered as
we danced, or while we held hands in the theatre, or while
dining at . . .
Caroline Stop it, Percy! Stop it!
Percy What's the matter? Are you telling me you didn't really
mean them?
Caroline It's the way I make my living. I'm not particularly proud

of it, and I won't bore you with the "poor childhood" bit, but there's one thing I learned very early on. Make full use of anything that's going for you.

Her hands indicate herself

So I use the one asset I've got—while it lasts.
Percy And to hell with the world eh?
Caroline It's the sort of world we live in.
Percy The world is what we make it.
Caroline Did you get me here to teach me your philosophy on life?
Percy Life? What life? I haven't got one. You stole it, remember?
Caroline What are you going to do?
Percy I'm going to bash your head in.

She is not particularly worried by this statement

Caroline Look Percy. For what it's worth, I'm sorry.
Percy That's worth nothing.
Caroline I'll give you your two thousand back, of course.
Percy That's worth even less.
Caroline If you don't want your money back, what do you want?
Percy I want to bash your head in.
Caroline Don't talk silly.

Percy just looks at her. She fiddles with her glass, frowning, annoyed

For goodness sake, Percy! Why is this such a big deal? I said you could have your money back . . .
Percy Money! You still don't understand, do you?
Caroline Look. Are you saying you didn't enjoy going out with me? Didn't I give you a good time?
Percy It was all false.
Caroline But you didn't know that then. I watched you. You were proud to be with me. I saw you preen when people looked at us. You can't deny that.
Percy You're right. It was wonderful. The most wonderful feeling I've ever had. I'll never forget it. I was so high.
Caroline There you are then.
Percy Which meant I had a hell of a way to fall!
Caroline Percy, listen. What I've done, I've done. I can't change that—but you mentioned feelings just now. Well, I have feelings too, and . . .

Percy Oh sure!

Caroline Yes, believe it or not—and I want you to know that when I was with you, they were very nice feelings.

Percy That's easy to say now.

Caroline It's true.

Percy True? What do you know about truth? Your whole life is one big lie.

Caroline I nearly didn't go through with it.

Percy Oh?

Caroline Most times it's easy—but with you, it was different. I really did enjoy your company. You didn't push, didn't presume. You were a —gentleman. I don't often meet that. I was very fond of you.

Percy So why did you . . .

Caroline I was scared of the consequences. You were changing me, and I couldn't afford to let you.

Percy You could have said—something.

Caroline Like what? "I really do like you, Percy, but I'm still going to take you for two thousand pounds"?

Percy Of course not—but we could . . .

She moves closer to him

Caroline I told you, you were different. I'm not really surprised you went to all this trouble to find me. It's just like you. In fact, in a way, I'm glad.

Percy Glad?

Caroline It gives me a chance to put things right—if you'll let me. Pay you back for all the hurt I've caused.

Percy Yes, it hurt. You'll never know how much it hurt.

She moves closer

Caroline I felt it, too. Let me make it up to you.

Percy You can't just undo all the . . .

She moves closer

Caroline I know. But we are here, now, together.

Percy How can I believe you—trust you . . .

She is now right in front of him

Caroline Percy—either bash my head in, or . . . (*She kisses him*)

Percy I want to believe you, but . . .
Caroline But nothing. (*She kisses him again*)

The kiss gets more passionate as Percy embraces her tightly, desperately. He speaks over her shoulder, still clutching her

Percy Don't ever go away again. Sweet Caroline. Never go away again. I love you—I love you! Please don't go . . .

Caroline soothes him

Caroline There, my love. I'm here. I'm not going anywhere.
Percy Do you promise? Promise me you mean it.
Caroline I promise—and I'll prove it.
Percy Prove it?
Caroline (*smiling*) You do have a bedroom here, don't you?
Percy Bedroom? Eh, yes, of course.
Caroline Then we have some catching up to do!
Percy Oh yes—Caroline. I love you so much.
Caroline And I love you, Percy. (*The kiss*) Thank you for giving me the chance to show you.

Percy breaks away, takes off his tie and sits Caroline down on the sofa

Percy Yowee! This calls for a celebration!
Caroline What sort of . . .
Percy Champagne!

He goes behind the sofa. Caroline turns, smiling

Caroline You've got champagne?
Percy Well, no. The wine will have to do!

They laugh. He bends over and kisses her. As she turns away, he flings the tie around her neck and pulls tight. Tighter and tighter as he talks to her

How does it feel, bitch! You thought you had won. You thought I believed you. How does it feel to lose, thinking you had won? How does it feel, bitch? I know how it feels. I . . . know . . . how . . . it . . .

She has been limp for some time. He slowly eases off, then throws the tie down. He goes to her handbag and takes out the gun. He sits next to her and puts her arms around his neck. He puts one arm around her shoulders. They are in a silent embrace. With his free arm, he raises the gun to his head, as

the CURTAIN *falls*

FURNITURE AND PROPERTY LIST

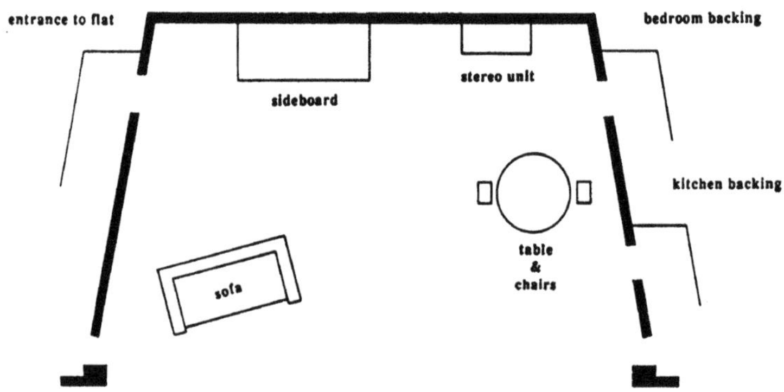

TO OPEN

On stage: Stereo unit
Sideboard. *On it:* telephone, telephone directory. *In it:* drinks,
glasses, pen, paper
Table
Two chairs
Two-seater sofa
Other items of furniture to set the scene—enough for disorder
to be created page 18, but see Production Notes

Off stage: Cup of tea: **(Mrs Yates)**
Newspaper **(Mrs Yates)**

Personal: **Percy:** overcoat, brief-case

Page 4—new "scene"

Off stage
  (bedroom): Shoes
                      Towel
                      Vest
                      Tie

  (kitchen): Shirt on hanger

Personal: **Mrs Yates**: duster
              Percy: overcoat. *In inside pocket*: letter; brief-case, newspaper

Page 8—new "scene"

On stage: Card on sideboard

Page 10—new "scene"

Off stage
  (bedroom): Gift-wrapped box of chocolates, tie

Personal: **Percy**: watch
              Caroline: handbag. *In it*: gun, handkerchief

Page 15—new "scene"

Off stage: **Mrs Yates**: two cups of tea

Page 18—new "scene"

Set: Wild disorder

Personal: **Percy**: newspaper

Page 20—new "scene"

Set: Living-room of new flat—see Production Notes

On stage: Sofa
              Table
              Two chairs

Personal: **Percy**: overcoat, brief-case. *In it*: writing paper, envelope

Page 20—new "scene"

On stage: On table: two drinks, two letters

Personal: **Percy:** watch, newspaper, horn-rimmed spectacles, tie
Caroline: handbag. *In it:* gun

LIGHTING PLOT

Interior settings: two simple living rooms

To open: General interior lighting—evening

Cue 1　**Percy:** "Man, forty-one, seeks female　　　(Page 4)
companion ..."
*Slow fade to Black-out. Then up to general interior
evening lighting*

Cue 2　**Mrs Yates** shrugs and exits　　　　　　(Page 8)
*Slow fade to Black-out. Then up to general interior
evening lighting*

Cue 3　**Mrs Yates** exits　　　　　　　　　　(Page 10)
*Slow fade to Black-out. Then up to general interior
evening lighting*

Cue 4　**Percy** and **Caroline** laugh, link arms and exit　(Page 15)
*Slow fade to Black-out. Then up to general interior
evening lighting*

Cue 5　**Percy** "Bitch! Bitch! Bitch! Bitch! Bitch!"　(Page 18)
*Slow fade to Black-out. Then up to general interior
morning lighting*

Cue 6　**Percy** "Yes—get away from it all"　　　(Page 20)
*Slow fade to Black-out. Then up to general interior
day-time lighting*

Cue 7　**Percy** "... Would like to meet female ..."　(Page 20)
*Slow fade to Black-out. Then up to general interior
lighting*

EFFECTS PLOT

Cue 1   As Curtain rises   (Page 1)
            Door slams

Cue 2   Lights come up   (Page 20)
            Door bell rings

MADE AND PRINTED IN GREAT BRITAIN BY
LATIMER TREND & COMPANY LTD PLYMOUTH

MADE IN ENGLAND